D1101438

ROSS & CROMARTY

NESS PUBLISHING

2   A Ross-shire panorama from Culbokie on the Black Isle looking west across the Cromarty Firth towards Maryburgh and Dingwall. Near the centre of the picture on the far side of the firth the

ROSS & CROMARTY

Hector Macdonald Memorial can just be made out, which is pictured on p.26. The peaks in the distance on the right are the Fannaich mountains, 25-30 miles away.

Welcome to Ross & Cromarty!

The old county of Ross & Cromarty stretches across northern Scotland from the town of Cromarty at the eastern tip of the Black Isle to Kyle of Lochalsh on the western coast. Between these extremities lies an area similar to that of Cyprus, in which can be found a range of scenery and settlements not easily bettered by any other part of Scotland. The charm of historic towns like Cromarty (opp.) is complemented by the awe-inspiring grandeur of mountains such as those of Inverpolly and Torridon.

As the name suggests, Ross & Cromarty was formed by the amalgamation of two counties in 1889. Although smaller, the county of Cromartyshire was the senior partner, originating in the 13th century. The amalgamation made more sense than some such arrangements because Cromarty comprised a number of pockets of territory dotted around Ross-shire, so that the two administrations were already well mixed in with each other. Today, Ross & Cromarty is part of Highland Region, but its name continues to be much in evidence even if its boundaries are no longer so clearly defined.

Ross & Cromarty has been home to its share of notable people. Maelrubha (642-722) founded the church in Applecross in 673 (see p.77) and was regarded as the patron saint of that part of

Looking down to Cromarty and the Cromarty Firth from the road to South Sutor.　5

6   On the other side of Scotland, but still in Ross & Cromarty, this view from Plockton looks over to Duncraig. The impressive crags provide the viewpoint for the picture on p.83.

cotland. Hugh Miller (1802-1856) is perhaps he greatest alumnus of more modern times to ome from the region. The Cromarty birthplace f this remarkable geologist, writer and church ader is open to visitors (see p.10).

This book takes readers on a tour of the ounty that starts in the east on the Black Isle nd goes around the Cromarty Firth to Tain efore striking north-west to Inverpolly. It then racks roughly south-west through a variety of oastal and inland locations such as Ullapool, Gairloch, Kinlochewe and Plockton before eaching the southernmost extremity of the ounty around Kintail.

This exploration shows the great variety that ums up Ross & Cromarty. Whether palm trees n Plockton, oil rigs in Nigg Bay, fishing ports ike Ullapool, inland seas like Loch Maree, red quirrels or golden eagles, each one makes its pecial contribution to this wonderful slice of Scotland.

One of several wynds (lanes) of attractive cottages in Cromarty.

8   The spit of land that is Chanonry Point stretches out into the Moray Firth from the south side of the Black Isle. A golf course occupies much of its length.

10 Left: Hugh Miller's cottage with the Miller House beyond. Right: Cromarty Courthouse, built 1773, is now a museum. The courtroom scene has life-like figures and soundtrack telling the story of a trial.

Cromarty harbour was developed in the 1770s to facilitate the import of raw material from the Baltic **11** to supply local cloth, ironware and rope factories. Today, a small ferry operates to Nigg.

12 Cromarty Lighthouse. It now serves as a Field Station for Aberdeen University's Institute of Biological and Environmental Sciences.

A modest walk from Cromarty goes south to some rugged coast where sea erosion has created 13
stacks, arches and caves like those seen here, known as McFarquhar's Bed.

14 The village of Rosemarkie, on the southern coast of the Black Isle, seen from Chanonry Point. This early settlement goes back to Pictish times – approximately the 3rd to 9th centuries.

Groam House Museum in Rosemarkie is dedicated to presenting and interpreting Pictish culture. **15** Displays are focused on 15 Pictish carved stones.

16 The ancient town of Fortrose lies just to the west of Rosemarkie. These attractive buildings are in the town centre on the northern side of the cathedral precincts.

Fortrose Cathedral was built in the 13th century by Bishop Robert of Ross. What remains today is only a small part of its original size – seen here are the south aisle and chapel.

18 Chanonry Point lighthouse. The name is derived from the nearby 'chanonry' cathedral in Fortrose. With the Fort George promontory opposite (see *Picturing Scotland: Inverness* in this series),

his is a narrow point on the Moray Firth that channels fish into shoals, making it a good feeding ground for the Moray Firth dolphins which can therefore often be seen here. 19

20 A few miles west of Fortrose, the village of Munlochy is situated at the head of this beautiful bay, an inlet on the north side of the Moray Firth.

North Kessock, just across the water from Inverness, gives tantalising views down the Beauly Firth to the distant mountains beyond. The building at bottom right is the Lifeboat Station.

22 Moving over to the north side of the Black Isle, this view illustrates its agricultural fertility. Inset: Seals can often be seen along the Cromarty Firth. This is a Common Seal.

Aerial pictures make good maps! Having explored the Black Isle on the right, we now come round 23
the head of the Cromarty Firth and make for Dingwall (on the left).

24 But first, a look at Ben Wyvis (1046m/3432ft) which dominates the area north of Dingwall and is seen here at sunrise. For those wishing to climb Ben Wyvis, the walk begins at a car park on the

A835 north of Garve and is approximately a nine-mile walk to the summit and back.

26 Left: the Town Hall (Tolbooth) and Museum in Dingwall, county town of Ross-shire. Right: the Memorial to Hector Macdonald, a local man who served in the Gordon Highlanders with distinction

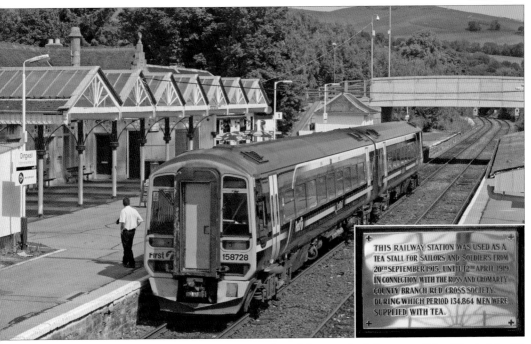

THIS RAILWAY STATION WAS USED AS A
TEA STALL FOR SAILORS AND SOLDIERS FROM
20TH SEPTEMBER 1915 UNTIL 12TH APRIL 1919
IN CONNECTION WITH THE ROSS AND CROMARTY
COUNTY BRANCH RED CROSS SOCIETY
DURING WHICH PERIOD 134,864 MEN WERE
SUPPLIED WITH TEA.

Dingwall is where the railway lines to the far north and the wonderfully scenic Kyle of Lochalsh **27**
route diverge. Inset: the plaque recalls First World War activity.

28 The railway lines may be long gone but the spa town of Strathpeffer has preserved its attractive Victorian station, which is home to shops and the Highland Museum of Childhood.

Strathpeffer Pavilion, opened in 1881, is a busy venue for the performing arts, weddings, exhibitions **29** and conferences. Inset: flowers by the Pavilion.

30 Castle Leod, just outside Strathpeffer. It has been home to the same family for 500 years. It is open to the public on selected days each year – see back of book for contact information.

The curious Fyrish Monument stands on a hilltop north of the Cromarty Firth. Built by General **31**
Sir Hector Munro, its design is said to be based on the gates of the Indian city of Nagapatnam.

32 From near the Fyrish Monument, a fine view east over the Cromarty Firth with the town of Invergordon in the middle distance. An oil rig is moored to the right, with Cromarty beyond.

Continuing east, Tarbat Discovery Centre is a museum situated in a church in Portmahomack. **33**
It is next to the site of the only Pictish monastery found in Scotland. Inset: Pictish Queen, Tarbat.

34 Portmahomack is situated on the Tarbat Peninsula and dates back to the arrival of St Colmac, who established a priory in 975. A lovely spot with views across the Dornoch Firth to Sutherland.

The easternmost tip of Ross & Cromarty is Tarbat Ness – the last few miles beyond Portmahomack. **35**
The low-lying nature of the land can be appreciated from this aerial view which looks south-west.

36 West of Tarbat Ness is the town of Tain. Its Collegiate Church was built between about 1370 and 1460 to house the shrine of St Duthac, an early medieval saint born in Tain.

A guest at a feast sent a piece of roast pork and a gold ring to Duthac's house. The messenger stopped at a kirkyard to rest and pray, and put the meat and the ring down on the ground. A kite swooped down and snatched them up, then flew away across a river into a forest. When Duthac was told of this, he concentrated his mind in prayer and the bird came to him. He retrieved the ring, but let it keep the meat.

A panel in Tain's excellent Pilgrimage Centre which illustrates and describes one of the miracles **37** credited to St Duthac. Tain has been a place of pilgrimage since at least the 14th century.

38 Tain was granted its first royal charter in 1066, making it Scotland's oldest Royal Burgh, an event commemorated in 1966 by the opening of this Rose Garden.

Founded in 1843, Glenmorangie Distillery in Tain has been pursuing perfection in making whisky **39** for over 160 years. It is open to visitors for tours and tastings.

40 Now we leap on nearly 50 miles to the northernmost part of Ross & Cromarty, the wilderness of
Inverpolly. On a still winter's day, the mountain of Cul Beag (769m/2523ft) is on the left, with Cul

Mor (849m/2785ft) on the right. In between, the summit of Stac Pollaidh can just be seen . . .

42 . . Stac Pollaidh is the area's most dramatic mountain and proves that being impressive is not just a matter of height – at 612m/2007ft it is not huge, but looks both crumbly and challenging.

For those who climb it, superb vistas like this await them. Cul Mor is seen again, looking a very **43** different shape compared with the view on p.41.

44 The ferry *Isle of Lewis* arrives at the port of Ullapool from Stornoway in the Outer Hebrides after a crossing of around two-and-three-quarter hours.

Ullapool is located on Loch Broom, south of Inverpolly. It was first laid out in 1788 by the British Fisheries Society and is still a fishing port. It also hosts the annual Loopallu Festival.

46 A closer view of Ullapool seafront. This attractive town is strategically placed to make it a good base from which to explore the area.

Looking south along Loch Broom soon after dawn, as the sunlight is just reaching the western **47** slopes. The distant mountains are the Fannaichs, first seen at even greater distance on p.3.

48 South of Ullapool, Loch Glascarnoch reflects Beinn Dearg (1084m/3556ft) on the right of the picture. Climbing it and two other nearby summits entails a walk of about 15 miles.

Loch Glascarnoch is drained by the Black Water which, some miles to the south, cascades over Rogie 49
Falls, seen here in winter spate. From here we head back to the north-west and more wild country.

50 To many, An Teallach is the most spectacular mountain on the Scottish mainland. To the left are the fearsome Corrag Buidhe pinnacles and to their right Sgurr Fiona summit (1060m/3478ft).

Now Corrag Buidhe and Sgurr Fiona are on the left, with An Teallach's highest summit, Bidean a' **51**
Ghlas Thuill (1062m/3484ft), in the centre above Loch Toll an Lochan.

52 The full traverse is one of the best expeditions in the country, not least because of the magnificent views it reveals. To the west is Loch Na Sealga with the Fisherfield Hills beyond.

To the north lies Corrie Hallie, starting point of one of the routes up An Teallach. For a view of the **53** whole mountain, see the back cover picture.

54 Continuing westwards for a few miles, the foaming waters of the Little Gruinard River flow from Fionn Loch and meet the sea at Gruinard Bay.

The glorious sands and wide-open space of Little Gruinard beach.

56 The A832 skirts a great wilderness as it loops its way through this region from Braemore Junction near Ullapool to Achnasheen. One of the best viewpoints is this classic Wester Ross panorama south

of Poolewe, with the length of Loch Maree stretching away on the right. In the distance on the left
re the Fisherfield Hills, first seen on p.52.

58 A different perspective on Little Gruinard beach – the name 'Gruinard' means shallow fjord or fjord of green water, which this picture bears out. For some places, 'idyllic' doesn't really cover it . . .

And now Gruinard Bay in winter, looking to the left of the picture opposite across the bay eastwards **59** to the distant mountains of Inverpolly. Beinn Mor Coigach is on the right.

60 The next stop along the west coast of Ross & Cromarty is Aultbea. Looking across the harbour provides a first glimpse of the Torridon skyline away to the south.

To complement the view *from* Aultbea, this scene looking north shows how the village is spread out 61 around the eastern bays of Loch Ewe.

62 One of the world's great gardens, Inverewe sprang from the vision and determination of Osgood Mackenzie. It is a National Trust for Scotland property.

Inverewe was founded in 1862 and is famed for its exotic plants, despite being further north than Moscow! This is the walled garden.

64 Loch Gairloch is a few miles west of Inverewe. Around its shores the village of the same name actually comprises a number of settlements – here we see the part known as Strath.

Gairloch harbour. Amongst many local attractions, Gairloch Heritage Museum stands out, taking
you on a journey through time showing how local people lived and worked through the ages.

66 Continuing south-east from Gairloch brings us to Loch Maree. This is one of the great Scottish lochs, 12 miles long and up to two miles wide. Beinn Airidh Charr rises beyond.

On a personal note, this picture of Loch Maree is a particular favourite. Taken from Letterewe Pier,
the composition, light and shade, plus Slioch sneaking into the top right corner, are a delight.

68 Further south along Loch Maree, mighty Slioch (981m/3218ft) really comes into its own, looking especially impressive in full winter mantle. Slioch is usually climbed from Kinlochewe.

For a preview of the next part of this tour we nip south to Achnasheen from where this 'taster' view **69** reveals Liathach and Beinn Eighe looming above the intervening landscape.

70 Left: Corrie Mhic Fhearchair's triple-buttress head wall on the eastern flank of Beinn Eighe is notably impressive. Right: Sgurr Ban summit, Beinn Eighe.

Beinn Eighe boasts two Munros (Scottish peaks higher than 3000ft), the higher of which is **71**
Ruadh-stac Mor (1010m/3314ft), pictured here.

72 Loch Torridon panorama. Taken from above Ardheslaig (in the foreground) on the Shieldaig to Applecross road, the view looks east towards the Torridon and Achnashellach mountains.

Liathach has its head in the clouds towards the left; Beinn Damh is the summit in shade on the right. The village of Shieldaig can be seen on the far waterline to the right.

74 Liathach, 'the grey one', is Torridon's most formidable mountain. Its five-mile ridge has eight separate tops, two of which are classified as Munros. The summit height is 1055m/3461ft.

West of Liathach is Beinn Alligin (986m/3235ft), its name meaning 'jewelled hill'. It's certainly a gem in terms of shapeliness and dramatic features, such as the Horns of Alligin at the central top.

76 The lovely village of Shieldaig was established in 1800, its name being derived from the Norse for 'herring bay'. Shieldaig and Loch Shieldaig can also be seen in the cover picture.

The Applecross peninsula is situated between Torridon and the sea. This is Applecross Bay with the village on the left and the Isle of Skye in the distance.

78 The 'main' road to Applecross traverses the notorious 610m/2000ft 'Bealach na Ba' (pass of the cattle) and is seen here disappearing into the void beneath the crags on the right.

Also pictured from the Bealach na Ba, this is the long-lens view down to the villages on the eastern side of Loch Kishorn, complete with some dramatic contrast due to cloud conditions.

80 Dawn lights up the village of Lochcarron. We are now south of Torridon and east of Applecross, the road to which can be seen on the hillside towards the right of the picture.

This picture is the reverse of the one opposite, i.e. looking across Loch Carron from the north **81** towards Plockton. Inset: otters can be seen on the shores around here.

82 Plockton is one of the most picturesque villages on the west coast of Ross & Cromarty. Its sheltered location and the influence of the Gulf Stream allow palm trees to grow.

A Plockton panorama looking north from Duncraig crags (see p.6). The village goes back to 1801, **83** this being the year in which plans for a settlement were drawn up.

84 A few more miles to the west bring us to romantic Kyle of Lochalsh, seen here from the approach to the Skye Bridge on a day of very mixed weather.

The ferry to Skye may have been replaced by the bridge, but other nautical adventures can be **85** undertaken, like a trip in a glass-bottomed boat such as *Seaprobe Atlantis*.

86 Eilean Donan Castle is on Loch Duich about seven miles east of Kyle of Lochalsh. The present-day castle was rebuilt from 1912 to 1932.

Eilean Donan is said to be the most-photographed castle in Scotland and given these two contrasting images it's not hard to see why. A castle has stood here since the early 13th century.

88 The scenic riches just keep coming! From the most-photographed castle it's only a few more miles on to one of Scotland's best-loved mountain views, the Five Sisters of Kintail. The Five Sisters are

the five tops from the centre to the right of the picture. Three of them are classified as Munros.

90 In the south-western corner of Ross & Cromarty, near Glenelg, are two remarkable survivors of Iron Age architecture: Dun Telve (above) and Dun Troddan (right) Brochs.

These strongholds stand about 10 metres high and incorporate a cavity-wall structure as can be seen above. They may originally have been roofed.

92 The Falls of Glomach, Kintail, are one of Scotland's highest and most dramatic waterfalls at around 115m/370ft. Reaching them entails a five-mile walk each way from Morvich, but well worth it!

Also in Kintail and overlooking the head of Loch Duich, A' Ghlas-bheinn (918m/3012ft) boasts a **93** summit ridge just made for scrambling!

94 The last leg through Ross & Cromarty is up Glen Shiel, hemmed in by mountains on each side. Looking back down the glen, a couple of these steep summits rise in the distance.

Journey's end is by Loch Cluanie, seen here in autumn. From here the land of Lochaber begins, **95** but that's another journey . . .

Published 2013 by Ness Publishing, 47 Academy Street, Elgin, Moray, IV30 1LR
Phone 01343 549663   www.nesspublishing.co.uk
(First edition published in 2008 entitled *Ross and Cromarty: a pictorial souvenir*)
All photographs © Colin and Eithne Nutt except pp.1, 4, 19, 22 (inset), 81 (inset) & 96 © Charlie Phillips; pp.23 & 35
© Scotavia Images; p.43 © Paul Turner

Text © Colin Nutt
ISBN 978-1-906549-35-0

Front cover: Loch Torridon towards Shieldaig; p.1: Pine Marten;
p.4: Red Squirrel; this page: Golden Eagle; back cover: An Teallach

For a list of websites and phone numbers please turn over > > > >

Websites and phone numbers (where available) for principal places featured in this book in alphabetical order:

Applecross Heritage Centre: www.applecrossheritage.org.uk
Aultbea: www.aultbea.camusnagaul.com
Beinn Eighe Nature Reserve: www.snh.org.uk (T) 01445 760254
Castle Leod: www.castleleod.org.uk (T) 01997 421264
Cromarty Courthouse: www.cromarty-courthouse.org.uk (T) 01381 600418
Dingwall Museum: www.dingwallmuseum.co.uk (T) 01349 865366
Dun Telve & Dun Troddan Brochs: www.historic-scotland.gov.uk
Eilean Donan Castle: www.eileandonancastle.com (T) 01599 555202
Falls of Glomach: www.nts.org.uk
Ferries from Ullapool: www.calmac.co.uk (T) 0800 066 5000
Fortrose Cathedral: www.historic-scotland.gov.uk (T) 01667 460232
Friends of the Kyle Line: www.kylerailway.co.uk (T) 01599 534824
Gairloch: www.gairloch.co.uk
Glenmorangie Distillery: www.glenmorangie.com/experience-perfection/distillery-tour (T) 01862 892477
Highland Museum of Childhood: www.highlandmuseumofchildhood.org.uk (T) 01997 421031
Hugh Miller Cottage and Museum: www.nts.org.uk (T) 0844 493 2158
Groam House Museum: www.groamhouse.org.uk (T) 01381 620961
Inverewe Garden: www.nts.org.uk (T) 0844 493 2225
Kintail: www.visitkintail.co.uk
Kyle of Lochalsh: www.lochalsh.co.uk
Plockton: www.plockton.com
Strathpeffer Pavilion: www.strathpefferpavilion.org.uk (T) 01997 420124
Tain Pilgrimage Centre: www.tainmuseum.org.uk (T) 01862 894089
Tarbat Discovery Centre: www.tarbat-discovery.co.uk (T) 01862 871361